Hello, Beautiful!

Farm Animals

WORLD BOOK

www.worldbook.com

World Book, Inc.
180 North LaSalle Street, Suite 900
Chicago, Illinois 60601
USA

For information about other World Book publications, visit our website at www.worldbook.com or call 1-800-WORLDBK (967-5325).

For information about sales to schools and libraries, call 1-800-975-3250 (United States), or 1-800-837-5365 (Canada).

Library of Congress Cataloging-in-Publication Data for this volume has been applied for.

Hello, Beautiful!
ISBN: 978-0-7166-3567-3 (set, hc.)

Farm Animals
ISBN: 978-0-7166-3571-0 (hc.)

Also available as:
ISBN: 978-0-7166-3581-9 (e-book)

Printed in China by Shenzhen Wing King Tong Paper Products Co., Ltd., Shenzhen, Guangdong
1st printing July 2018

Staff

Writer: Grace Guibert

Executive Committee

President
Jim O'Rourke

Vice President and
Editor in Chief
Paul A. Kobasa

Vice President, Finance
Donald D. Keller

Vice President, Marketing
Jean Lin

Vice President,
International Sales
Maksim Rutenberg

Vice President, Technology
Jason Dole

Director, Human Resources
Bev Ecker

Editorial

Director, New Print
Tom Evans

Managing Editor, New Print
Jeff De La Rosa

Senior Editor, New Print
Shawn Brennan

Editor, New Print
Grace Guibert

Librarian
S. Thomas Richardson

Manager, Contracts &
Compliance (Rights &
Permissions)
Loranne K. Shields

Manager, Indexing Services
David Pofelski

Digital

Director, Digital Content
Development
Emily Kline

Director, Digital Product
Development
Erika Meller

Manager, Digital Products
Jonathan Wills

Graphics and Design

Senior Art Director
Tom Evans

Senior Visual
Communications Designer
Melanie Bender

Media Researcher
Rosalia Bledsoe

Manufacturing/ Production

Manufacturing Manager
Anne Fritzinger

Proofreader
Nathalie Strassheim

Contents

Introduction

Welcome to "Hello, Beautiful!" picture books!

This book is about animals you might find on a farm. Each book in the "Hello, Beautiful!" series uses large, colorful photographs and a few words to describe our world to children who are not yet reading on their own or are beginning to learn to read. For the benefit of both grown-up and child readers, a picture key is included in the back of the volume to describe each photograph and specific type of animal in more detail.

"Hello, Beautiful!" books can help pre-readers and starting readers get into the habit of having fun with books and learning from them, too. With pre-readers, a grown-up reader (parent, grandparent, librarian, teacher, older brother or sister) can point to the words on each page as he or she speaks them aloud to help the listening child associate the concept of text with the object or idea it describes.

Large, colorful photographs give pre-readers plenty to see while they listen to the reader. If no reader is available, pre-readers can "read" on their own, turning the pages of the book and speaking their own stories about what they see. For new readers, the photographs provide visual hints about the words on the page. Often, these words describe the specific type of animal shown. This animal may not be representative of all species, or types, of that animal.

This book displays some of the friendly faces of common farm animals. Help inspire respect and care for these important and beautiful animals by sharing this "Hello, Beautiful!" book with a child soon.

Chicken

Hello, beautiful chicken!

You are a barred Plymouth Rock hen.

You have a piece of red skin on the top of your head. It looks like a comb!

You are a female chicken. You lay eggs for people to eat.

Cow

Hello, beautiful cow!

Mooooooo! You are a Holstein cow. You are **black** and white.

You eat grass all day! You make lots of milk for us to drink.

Duck

Hello, beautiful duck!

You are a Muscovy duck. You have a red, warty mask around your eyes when you are grown up.

You are helpful on the farm. You eat bugs!

Goat

Hello, beautiful goat!

You are an Alpine goat. You have **brown** hair and light stripes on each side of your face.

Farmers raise you for your good milk!

Goose

Hello, beautiful goose!

Honk! Honk! You are an Embden goose. You guard the farm!

You have soft, warm feathers. You are happy on land or in water!

Hog

Hello, beautiful hog!

You are a Berkshire hog. You use your flat nose to dig around for food.

You roll in the mud to stay cool!

Horse

Hello,
beautiful horse!

You are a Percheron horse.
Your long legs make you a
fast runner. You are strong
enough to pull a plow and
help with farm work!

18

Llama

Hello, beautiful llama!

You are a woolly llama. Your long hair is very soft!

You can help carry heavy loads up and down hills and mountains.

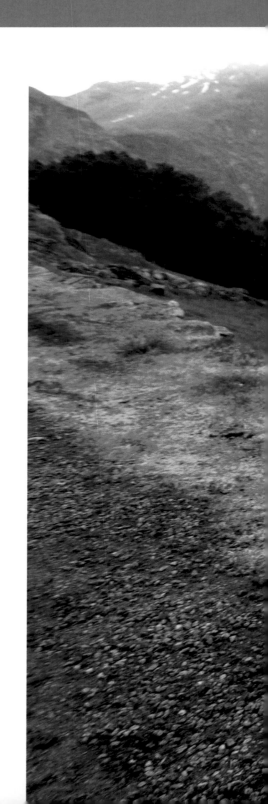

Rabbit

Hello, beautiful rabbit!

You are a New Zealand rabbit. You have long ears, a short tail, and soft fur.

There always are lots of baby rabbits on the farm!

Rooster

Hello, beautiful rooster!

You are a **brown** leghorn rooster. You are a male chicken. You have bright, colorful feathers.

You might wake up
farmers when you shout
cock-a-doodle-do!

Sheep

Hello, beautiful sheep!

Baaaaaaaaaah!
You are a Corriedale sheep.

You have a coat of soft, warm wool. Some farmers raise you just for it!

Turkey

Hello, beautiful turkey!

Gobble-gobble! You are a bronze turkey.

Male turkeys like you have a reddish head and neck. You are too big to fly around on the farm!

Picture Key

Learn more about these farm animals! Use the picture keys below to learn where each animal comes from, how big each animal grows, and what each animal eats!

Chicken

Hello, beautiful chicken!

You are a barred Plymouth Rock hen.

You have a piece of red skin on the top of your head. It looks like a comb!

You are a female chicken. You lay eggs for people to eat.

Cow

Mooooooooo!

Hello, beautiful cow!

Mooooooooo! You are a Holstein cow. You are **black** and **white**.

You eat grass all day! You make lots of milk for us to drink.

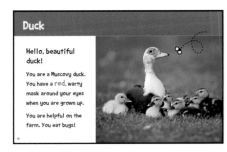

Duck

Hello, beautiful duck!

You are a Muscovy duck. You have a red, warty mask around your eyes when you are grown up.

You are helpful on the farm. You eat bugs!

Pages 6-7 Chicken

The barred Plymouth Rock chicken was bred in the United States. These birds grow to about 7 ½ pounds (3.40 kilograms). Farmers give their chickens a special feed that provides nutrients to help them grow.

Pages 8-9 Cow

The Holstein (*HOHL styn* or *HOHL steen*) cow is sometimes called the Holstein-Friesian cow. It originated in the province of Friesland in the Netherlands. Cattle raisers of the Schleswig-Holstein region of Germany also helped develop the breed. It is now among the most common in the world. The cow weighs about 1,500 pounds (680 kilograms). *Bulls* (male cattle) often weigh even more. Cows may feed on grass or be given special feed by farmers.

Pages 10-11 Duck

The Muscovy (*MUHS kuh vee*) duck is native to Mexico, Central America, and South America. They are commonly farmed all across North America. Male domesticated Muscovy ducks can reach 10 to 15 pounds (4.5 to 7 kilograms). Females are smaller. Farmers may give their ducks pre-made feed that provides protein, grain, and other nutrients. Some farmers give their ducks fresh greens, worms, and corn.

Goat

Hello, beautiful goat!

You are an Alpine goat. You have **brown** hair and light stripes on each side of your face.

Farmers raise you for your good milk!

Goose

Hello, beautiful goose!

Honk! Honk! You are an Embden goose. You guard the farm!

You have soft, warm feathers. You are happy on land or in water!

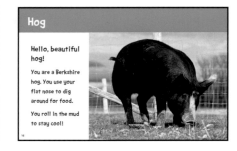

Hog

Hello, beautiful hog!

You are a Berkshire hog. You use your flat nose to dig around for food.

You roll in the mud to stay cool!

Pages 12-13 Goat

The Alpine goat originated in the mountains of the French Alps. Adults weigh up to 130 pounds (60 kilograms). They eat grain and hay. *Kids,* or baby goats, need lots of milk to help them grow.

Pages 14-15 Goose

The Embden (*EHM duhn*) goose originated in Embden, Germany. It is the tallest goose. It can reach 3 ⅓ feet (1 meter) in height. Embden geese weigh from about 20 to 30 pounds (9 to 14 kilograms). Males are larger than females. Farmers feed their geese special food to promote rapid growth. The feed consists of such ingredients as grain, soybean meal, meat by-products, vitamins, and minerals.

Pages 16-17 Hog

The Berkshire (*BURK shihr*) hog originated in Berkshire, England. Adult Berkshire hogs weigh about 600 pounds (270 kilograms). Farmers feed hogs well-balanced diets to help them grow. Hogs eat grains and meats.

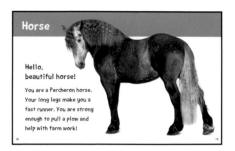

Pages 18-19 Horse

The Percheron (*PUR chuh ron*) horse was probably bred in Perche, France, in the Middle Ages (A.D. 400's through the 1400's). They measure 15 to 17 hands (60 to 68 inches, 150 to 173 centimeters) from the ground to the highest point of the *withers* (ridge between the shoulder bones). Horses eat grass, grain, and hay. They need about 2 ounces (57 grams) of salt daily to replenish what they sweat out.

Pages 20-21 Llama

Woolly llamas (*LAH muhz*) are native to South America. Adults measure about 4 feet (1.2 meters) tall at the shoulder. They eat the grasses and low shrubs that grow on the mountains where they live.

Pages 22-23 Rabbit

Despite its name, the New Zealand rabbit originated in the United States. They grow to about 10 pounds (4.5 kilograms). They eat leafy plants and food pellets.

Pages 24-25 Rooster

The brown leghorn chicken originated in Tuscany, on the west coast of Italy. It was named for the Tuscan seaport of Livorno, sometimes called Leghorn. A brown leghorn rooster grows to be about 6 pounds (2.7 kilograms). Like hens, roosters are given a special feed with nutrients to help them grow.

Pages 26-27 Sheep

The Corriedale (*KAWR ee dayl* or *KOR ee dayl*) sheep is native to Australia and New Zealand. Mature *rams* (males) weigh from 175 to 275 pounds (80 to 125 kilograms). *Ewes* (females) weigh from 130 to 180 pounds (60 to 80 kilograms). Sheep graze on range grasses.

Pages 28-29 Turkey

Bronze turkeys were first bred in the 1700's by crossing English turkeys with the wild turkey of North America. They are among the most commonly farmed breeds across the United States. The bird is the largest domestic American turkey. Adults weigh up to 50 pounds (23 kilograms). Farmers give their turkeys special food to help them grow.

Index